Caterpillar

Pocket

Guide

Edited by
Bob LaVoie

Iconografix

Iconografix, Inc.
PO Box 446
Hudson, Wisconsin 54016 USA

Iconografix books are offered at a discount when sold in quantity for promotional use. Businesses or organizations seeking details should write to the Marketing Department, Iconografix, at the above address.

Library of Congress Card Number: 99-76044

ISBN 1-58388-022-4

00 01 02 03 04 05 06 5 4 3 2 1

Printed in the United States of America

Cover and book design by Shawn Glidden

Book Proposals

Iconografix is a publishing company specializing in books for transportation enthusiasts. We publish in a number of different areas, including Automobiles, Auto Racing, Buses, Construction Equipment, Emergency Equipment, Farming Equipment, Railroads & Trucks. The Iconografix imprint is constantly growing and expanding into new subject areas.

Authors, editors, and knowledgeable enthusiasts in the field of transportation history are invited to contact the Editorial Department at Iconografix, Inc., PO Box 446, Hudson, WI 54016.

Table of Contents

Dedication

To Teather

Acknowledgments

I wish to thank the Business Resource Center of Caterpillar, Inc. for their continued support of my projects.

I also sincerely thank my friends at Iconografix, Inc. for undertaking this new project and for their patience and continued support.

Finally, I wish to thank Peter Longfoot for supplying difficult to obtain photos.

Introduction

When the Caterpillar Tractor Co. was formed in 1925, they kept only three machines in their product line. Held over from the Holt line was the 2-ton to fill the small tractor void. In the medium and large tractor areas the old Best Thirty and Sixty models remained.

In 1927 the "L" series Twenty was introduced as the first totally new machine designed by the new company. The production of the "L" Twenty began in San Leandro and in 1928 production of the "PL" Twenty began in Peoria. In 1928 the Ten and PV Fifteen were introduced and the 2-ton was discontinued.

In July of 1931 the Twenty Five was introduced and it finally replaced the "PL" Twenty in December of 1931 in the product line. A skip occurred in the PL Twenty serial number run between PL6319 and PL6587. This is a span of 268 tractors, which is the same number of model Twenty Five tractors produced in 1931. Since the Twenty Five was introduced to replace the "PL" Twenty, it seems the early model Twenty Five tractors shared the missing numbers in the "PL" Twenty run. It is likely that Twenty Five tractors made from July of 1931 up to the December 7, 1931 paint change were painted gray.

In 1932 the 7C Fifteen was introduced to replace the Ten. The 1D series High Fifteen replaced the High Ten. Also, in 1932 the 8C Twenty replaced the PV Fifteen and it is possible an 8C Twenty High Clearance was produced.

The Thirty Five was also introduced in 1932 taking up the medium size tractor space. In 1933 the Twenty Eight replaced the Twenty Five. In 1934 the Forty replaced the Thirty Five. The Fifty was introduced in 1931 and produced with limited yearly production until it was discontinued in 1937.

The Twenty Two was introduced in 1934 and became the most popular small gas tractor for the company. It replaced the 8C Twenty.

With production of the D9900 engine and the Diesel Sixty, a new age of diesels was born. The Diesel Seventy was produced in limited numbers in 1933.

Later, the diesels Thirty Five, Forty, Fifty, and Seventy Five were produced, filling all ranges of the product line. The RD series diesel tractors replaced the numbered series machines after that.

During the late 1930s and 1940s the R series gas tractors were produced following the long running model Twenty Two and 6G Thirty.

Eventually all gas tractors would fall to the new diesels and the D2 through D9 became the mainstay of the product line. The "D" designation remains today in identifying the track-type tractors produced.

- -

The information contained in the following pages has been culled from numerous sources and represents the most accurate information available. For some of the models presented information is very sketchy and in some cases contradictory. In those cases the author attempted to resolve the differences and present the most widely accepted data.

NUMBERED GAS TRACTORS

Model Ten

In late 1928, Caterpillar Tractor Company unveiled the Model Ten tractor. Weighing in at 4,500 pounds, it was the smallest tractor to be made by the company and, at the time, filled a gap in the small crawler-tractor marketplace. Unfortunately, the Model Ten was born with design problems, and from early on, its future was dim. When the tractor was discontinued in 1932, only 4,929 units had been made. The tractor was available in standard gauge (or narrow-gauge) at 37 inches, wide-gauge at 44 inches, an orchard or tail seat version in both gauges and a high clearance model. The standard high clearance Ten was a 44 inch gauge. This is the same gauge width as the wide-gauge low Ten. It is unclear how many versions were made. All variations of the Model Ten carried the "PT" serial number prefix, and no additional designations were issued to the special units.

Model Ten

Serial Numbers ....PT 1 - PT 4929
Manufacture Dates .... 12/14/28 - 12/4/32
Weight (lb.) 4420
Gauges .... 44 inch / 37 inch
Drawbar horsepower 15
Belt/PTO horsepower 19
Cylinders - Bore and stroke (in.) .... 4 @ 3 3/8 x 4
R.P.M. 1500
Nebraska test number 160
Fuel tank capacity (gal.) 17.5
Final drive capacity (qt.) 3
Transmission capacity (qt.) 6
Crankcase capacity (qt.) 7
Cooling system capacity (gal.) 4
Grouser shoe height .... 1 3/4 inch
Sprocket R.P.M. (2nd gear) 35
Valve clearance (hot) in .000" 8
Magneto points clearance in .000" 12
Options/Versions .... High Clearance, Wide, Orchard
Paint color .... Grey, Yellow after 12/7/31

Fifteen 7C Series

In 1932, Caterpillar introduced two "new" redesigned machines. The modifications made to the tractors were all lessons learned from the model Ten and PV Fifteen. The new tractors, known as the 8C Twenty, or small Twenty, and the 7C Fifteen, or small Fifteen, incorporated new technology that was to be used for several years. The small Fifteen was also available in an orchard (or tail seat) model and the high clearance model. The high clearance model was produced in the 44 inch gauge. The high clearance Fifteen was the first version of a model to be given its own serial number. This variation was issued the serial number 1D. All units from 1D1 to 1D95 were definitely high clearance machines and required those special parts.

Fifteen 7C Series

Serial Numbers .... 7C1 - 7C307
1D1 - 1D95 (High Clearance)
Manufacture Dates .... 3/31/32 - 11/17/33
Weight (lb.) 4480
Gauges .... 44 inch / 37 inch
Drawbar horsepower 15
Belt/PTO horsepower 18
Cylinders - Bore and stroke (in.) .... 4 @ 3 3/8 x 4
R.P.M. 1500
Nebraska test number 207
Fuel tank capacity (gal.) 17.5
Final drive capacity (qt.) 3
Transmission capacity (qt.) 6
Crankcase capacity (qt.) 7
Cooling system capacity (gal.) 4
Grouser shoe height .... 1 3/4 inch
Sprocket R.P.M. (2nd gear) 35
Valve clearance (hot) in .000". 8
Magneto points clearance in .000" 12
Options/Versions ..... High Clearance (1D), Wide, Orchard
Paint color .... Yellow

Model Fifteen PV Series

In 1929, Caterpillar introduced the model Fifteen PV Series. The tractor was similar to the model Ten in design, but on a larger scale. The tractor was produced until 1932 with a total production of 7,559 units.

The big Fifteen is common to several models. It has the design of a Ten, the same main mechanical components as a Small 8C Twenty, and the same undercarriage as a Twenty Two. However, it should not be mistaken with the 7C small Fifteen.

The tractor was available in narrow (or standard) gauge at 40 inches and wide-gauge at 50 inches. An orchard version was available in both gauges and is the rarest of the three styles. The orchard tractor (or tail seat) is equipped with full fenders, a lowered implement style seat, and a hand clutch. They are found in limited to moderate numbers on the West Coast. It is unknown how many orchard Fifteen tractors were made, but my guess is less than 1,000.

Model Fifteen PV Series

Serial Numbers	PV1 - PV7559
Manufacture Dates	1929 - 1932
Weight (lb.)	5790
Gauges	50 inch / 40 inch
Drawbar horsepower	22
Belt/PTO horsepower	26
Cylinders - Bore and stroke (in.)	4 @ 3 3/4 X 5
R.P.M.	1250
Nebraska test number	159
Fuel tank capacity (gal.)	23
Final drive capacity (qt.)	4
Transmission capacity (qt.)	8
Crankcase capacity (qt.)	10
Cooling system capacity (gal.)	4 3/4
Grouser shoe height	1 7/8
Tracklink height	3
Roller outer flange O.D.	8
Roller inner flange O.D.	7 7/8
O.D. Rolling surface sprocket	7
Sprocket R.P.M. (2nd gear)	35.7
Valve clearance (hot) in .000"	8
Magneto points clearance in .000"	12
Options/Versions	Wide, Orchard
Paint color	Grey, Yellow after 12/7/31

Model Twenty L & PL Series

In 1927, two years after the formation of the Caterpillar Tractor Company, the Model Twenty was introduced. This tractor was the first totally new tractor to be manufactured by the company. In many respects, the Twenty borrowed much of its engineering from its big brother, the Thirty, which was a huge success.

The Twenty was first manufactured in the San Leandro, California plant. Later in 1928, production increased and when production of the Twenty ended in 1931, a total of 6,319 units had been manufactured. It should also be noted that in 1931, a special order for 12 Model Twenty tractors was placed and numbers PL6587 through PL6598 were produced. It is not known why there is a gap between the two production runs or where these last 12 tractors went. Perhaps it is more than a coincidence that if you subtract the ending number of 6319 from the first number after the break, 6587, you get 268. This is the exact number of model Twenty Five tractors made in 1931. Also at serial number 268 the Twenty Five took on a new look to become less like the model Twenty it replaced.

As with most other tractors of this era, the Twenty was available in several variations; the most common version is the 42 inch narrow-gauge, which is found in most areas of the country. This model

Model Twenty L & PL Series

was used by farmers and loggers, as well as in small construction applications. It was available in a tail seat (or orchard) model in both gauges. These seem to be found in fair numbers in the orchard areas of the West Coast.

The wide-gauge model is the most scarce. Unlike the wide-gauge Model Ten and Fifteen, the Twenty did not have the concave rear sprocket. Instead, a spacer was placed between the rear-end housing of the tractor and the final drive housing. The main spring was also larger, giving the tractor its 55 inch wide-gauge. The Twenty wide-gauge was also made into a tail seat orchard model. These are very rare and sought after by collectors.

Serial Numbers .... L1 - L 1970, PL1 - PL6319,
PL6587 - PL6598
Manufacture Dates .... 11/1/27 - 9/30/31
Weight (lb.) 7740
Gauges .... 55 inch / 42 inch
Drawbar horsepower 28
Belt/PTO horsepower 31
Cylinders - Bore and stroke (in.) .... 4 @ 4 X 5 1/2
R.P.M. 1100
Nebraska test number 150
Fuel tank capacity (gal.) 25
Final drive capacity (qt.) 4
Transmission capacity (qt.) 8
Crankcase capacity (qt.) 11
Cooling system capacity (gal.) 5.5
Grouser shoe height 1 7/8
Sprocket R.P.M. (2nd gear) 32
Valve clearance (hot) in .000" 9
Magneto points clearance in .000" 12
Options/Versions .... Wide, Orchard
Paint color .... Grey, Yellow after 12/7/31

Model Twenty 8C Series

In 1932, while the model Ten became the 7C Fifteen, the PV Fifteen was transformed into the model Twenty 8C Series. The 8C Twenty was given several names to differentiate it from the old model Twenty in the L and PL series. The only thing similar between the two is their name. The 8C Twenty is also known as the Small Twenty and the Flathead Twenty.

The 8C is important for several reasons. Most important is that it is a transition model from the PV Fifteen to the model Twenty Two. Also, along with the 7C Fifteen, it was the first totally redesigned tractor to be painted the new Highway Yellow color with the black lettering and decals. The model Twenty Five was painted yellow in 1931 when it was introduced, but at that time it was really just a PL Twenty with a different name. The C Series Tractors were the first to undergo a major change and to be painted a new color.

The 8C, like the 7C, was given a new smart design. All the problems from the PV Fifteen were remedied, even though the main components of the tractor were kept the same. The changes were

Model Twenty 8C Series

mainly in appearance and design. The problems that the 7C solved for the Model Ten were the same ones the 8C solved for the PV Fifteen. The 8C Twenty was also available as an orchard model and possibly a high clearance.

Serial Numbers .... 8C1 - 8C652
Manufacture Dates .... 2/9/32 - 1/16/34
Weight (lb.) 5933
Gauges .... 50 inch / 40 inch
Drawbar horsepower 23
Belt/PTO horsepower 28
Cylinders - Bore and stroke (in.) .... 4 @ 3 3/4 X 5
R.P.M. 1250
Nebraska test number 205
Fuel tank capacity (gal.) 24.5
Final drive capacity (qt.) 4
Transmission capacity (qt.) 8
Crankcase capacity (qt.) 10
Cooling system capacity (gal.) 4 3/4
Grouser shoe height 1 7/8
Tracklink height 3
Roller outer flange O.D. 8
O.D. Rolling surface sprocket 7
Sprocket R.P.M. (2nd gear) 41
Valve clearance (hot) in .000" 8
Magneto points clearance in .000" 12
Options/Versions .... Wide, Orchard
Paint color .... Yellow

Model Twenty Two

In 1934, Caterpillar introduced the Model Twenty Two. When production ceased in 1939, a total of 9,999 2F (or First Series) and 5,157 1J Series, were produced. Using a 26-horsepower, 4 x 5 inch OHV engine and a new updated design, the Twenty Two was the company's most successful small gas crawler.

The Twenty Two was available in 40 inch standard gauge with convex rear sprockets, 50 inch wide-gauge with concave rear sprockets and an orchard-equipped model. All variations of the Model Twenty Two seem to be in good supply. The orchard models are found generally on the West Coast but are still fairly common throughout the United States. Many are still in use today. A high clearance wide-gauge was also offered. (See High Clearance appendix.)

Model Twenty Two

Serial Numbers .... 2F1 - 2F9999, 1J1 - 1J5155
Manufacture Dates .... 1/19/34 - 8/30/39
Weight (lb.) 6210
Gauges .... 50 inch / 40 inch
Drawbar horsepower 25
Belt/PTO horsepower 31
Cylinders - Bore and stroke (in.) .... 4@ 4 X 5
R.P.M. 1250
Nebraska test number 220
Fuel tank capacity (gal.) 22
Final drive capacity (qt.) 4
Transmission capacity (qt.) 8
Crankcase capacity (qt.) 10
Cooling system capacity (gal.) 5
Grouser shoe height 1 7/8
Tracklink height 3
Roller outer flange O.D. 8
O.D. Rolling surface sprocket 7
Sprocket R.P.M. (2nd gear) 35.7
Valve clearance (hot) in .000" 12
Magneto points clearance in .000" 20
Options/Versions .... Wide, Orchard, High Clearance
Paint color .... Yellow

Model Twenty Five

On December 7, 1931, the Caterpillar Model Twenty tractor was re-designated as the Model Twenty Five tractor. Like the Twenty, the Twenty Five still produced 28 horsepower. Basically, the two tractors were the same except for the radiator side plates, and in the later Model Twenty Five, the fenders were changed and there were other slight modifications.

When production ended in 1933, only 638 units had been produced. This tractor, in wide-gauge at 55 inches, narrow-gauge at 42 inches and tail seat versions, is one of the most sought by collectors.

Since the Model Twenty Five is nearly identical to the PL Model Twenty, most parts are interchangeable. On the early Model Twenty Five, the curved rear fenders were used, as on the Twenty. About the last 400 Model Twenty Five tractors had straight fenders. The later models also had a slightly different exhaust manifold.

The Twenty Five production started in June of 1931 making some of the early tractors gray. It is also interesting that 268 model Twenty Five tractors were made in 1931. This is the same number of tractors skipped in the ending group of PL Twenty serial numbers. The skip occurred from PL6319 to PL6587, 268 units. Some Twenty Five tractors have been found with a 3C number on the rear end and a PL number within the skip in the PL numbering system. The early Twenty

Model Twenty Five

Five tractors made in 1931 were initially equipped with engines in the PL Twenty skip. It is not known how many used the different engine number but a few examples are known and the 3C number matches in order the PL number in the skip. Example 3C4 has engine PL6323, four numbers into the skip.

Serial Numbers .... 3C1 - 3C638
Manufacture Dates .... 6/11/31 - 9/12/33
Weight (lb.) 7700
Gauges .... 55 inch / 42 inch
Drawbar horsepower 28
Belt/PTO horsepower 35
Cylinders - Bore and stroke (in.) .... 4 @ 4 X 5 1/2
R.P.M. 1100
Nebraska test number 203
Fuel tank capacity (gal.) 25
Final drive capacity (qt.) 4
Transmission capacity (qt.) 8
Crankcase capacity (qt.) 11
Cooling system capacity (gal.) 5.5
Grouser shoe height 2
Sprocket R.P.M. (2nd gear) 32
Valve clearance (hot) in .000" 9
Magneto points clearance in .000" 12
Options/Versions .... Wide, Orchard
Paint color .... Grey, Yellow after 12/7/31

Model Twenty Eight

In 1933, Caterpillar gave Models Twenty and Twenty Five another update with the Model Twenty Eight. When production of the Model Twenty Eight ended in 1935, only 1,171 units had been produced. The Model Twenty Eight was marketed in standard-gauge at 42 inches, wide-gauge at 55 inches and an orchard model.

As shown by the relatively low number produced, the Twenty Eight is moderately rare. The wide-gauge and orchard models are more rare than the standard version. It is not known how many of these special variations were made, but they seem as scarce as with many other models.

Model Twenty Eight

Serial Numbers .... 4F1 - 4F1171
Manufacture Dates .... 12/4/33 - 11/11/35
Weight (lb.) 7830
Gauges .... 55 inch / 42 inch
Drawbar horsepower 30
Belt/PTO horsepower 37
Cylinders - Bore and stroke (in.) .... 4 @ 4 3/16 X 5 1/2
R.P.M. 1100
Fuel tank capacity (gal.) 25
Final drive capacity (qt.) 4
Transmission capacity (qt.) 8
Crankcase capacity (qt.) 11
Cooling system capacity (gal.) 6
Grouser shoe height 1 7/8
Sprocket R.P.M. (2nd gear) 32
Valve clearance (hot) in .000" 15
Magneto points clearance in .000" 12
Options/Versions .... Wide, Orchard
Paint color .... Yellow

Model Thirty S & PS Series

When the Caterpillar Tractor Company was formed in 1925, the Model Thirty was held over from the Best Tractor Company product line. The Model Thirty was first produced in 1921 in the S Series and continued until 1932 when it was discontinued as the PS Series. This is covering the Model Thirty of post-1925 production.

The Model S tractors were produced in the San Leandro, California plant until 1930, with production ending at serial number S10536. This indicates that approximately 7,000 Model S Thirtys were produced under the Caterpillar name from 1925 to 1930. The PS Series tractors were made from 1927 until 1932 at the Peoria, Illinois plant with a total production of 14,294 machines. The Model Thirty was a successful tractor for both Best and later, Caterpillar.

The Thirty was available in standard (or narrow-gauge) at 43 3/4 inches, wide-gauge at 60 3/4 inches and an orchard model. The wide-gauge version is the rarest of the three styles and the orchard is next. The standard Thirty is in good supply in most areas of the country. The orchard style is most generally found on the West Coast and in moderate numbers.

Model Thirty S & PS Series

The Thirty's engine is a 4 3/4 inch bore by 6 1/2 inch stroke, valve-in-head, producing 25 drawbar horsepower and 30 belt horsepower. Shipping weight of the tractor was approximately 10,000 pounds.

Serial Numbers .... S1001 - S10536, PS1 - PS14294
Manufacture Dates .... 7/1/25 - 10/4/32
Weight (lb.) 9910
Gauges .... 60 3/4 inch / 43 3/4 inch
Drawbar horsepower 35
Belt/PTO horsepower 40
Cylinders - Bore and stroke (in.) .... 4 @ 4 3/4 X 6 1/2
R.P.M. 850
Nebraska test number 104
Fuel tank capacity (gal.) 37
Final drive capacity (qt.) 6
Transmission capacity (qt.) 20
Crankcase capacity (qt.) 20
Cooling system capacity (gal.) 11
Grouser shoe height 2
Sprocket R.P.M. (2nd gear) 31
Valve clearance (hot) in .000" 15
Magneto points clearance in .000" 18
Options/Versions .... Wide, Orchard
Paint color .... Grey, Yellow after 12/7/31

Model Thirty 6G Series/R4

In 1935, a totally redesigned Model Thirty was introduced in the 6G Series. This model was introduced three years after the old PS Series Thirty was discontinued, and it had a totally new look. Only 874 units were produced carrying the Thirty name. After that, the model was re-designated as the Model R4. The tractor weighed in at just over 9,000 pounds.

The tractors were available in narrow (or standard-gauge) at 44 inches, wide-gauge at 60 inches and the orchard-equipped model. All variations of the machines carrying the Thirty name over the radiator are quite rare and sought after. The R4 designated machines are far more common and are found in most areas. Total production of both machines combined was 5,383 units, with 4,508 units carrying the R4 designation.

Model Thirty 6G Series/R4

Serial Numbers .... 6G1 - 6G5383
Manufacture Dates .... 12/11/35 - 12/31/42
Weight (lb.) 9390
Gauges .... 60 inch / 44 inch
Drawbar horsepower 35
Belt/PTO horsepower 40
Cylinders - Bore and stroke (in.) .... 4 @ 4 1/4 X 5 1/2
R.P.M. 1400
Nebraska test number 272
Fuel tank capacity (gal.) 32
Final drive capacity (qt.) 7
Transmission capacity (qt.) 20
Crankcase capacity (qt.) 14
Cooling system capacity (gal.) 11
Grouser shoe height 2
Tracklink height 3 5/16
Roller outer flange O.D. 9 5/8
Roller inner flange O.D. 8 15/16
O.D. Rolling surface sprocket 8
Sprocket R.P.M. (2nd gear) 27
Valve clearance (hot) in .000" 10
Magneto points clearance in .000" 20
Options/Versions .... Wide, Orchard
Paint color .... Yellow

Model Thirty Five

In 1932, the Model Thirty Five tractor was introduced to fill the void left by the Model Thirty PS Series. The tractor was equipped with basically the same engine and undercarriage as the old Thirty but was given a more up-to-date look. When production ended in 1934, only 1,728 machines had been made.

The Thirty Five was available in narrow (or standard-gauge) at 56 inches, wide-gauge at 74 inches and an orchard model.

The 4 7/8 x 6 1/2 inch four-cylinder engine produced 38 drawbar horsepower. Weighing in at 12,480 pounds, it was slightly heavier than the Model Thirty that it replaced.

Model Thirty Five

Serial Numbers .... 5C1 - 5C1728
Manufacture Dates .... 2/29/32 - 10/29/34
Weight (lb.) 12480
Gauges .... 74 inch / 56 inch
Drawbar horsepower 38
Belt/PTO horsepower 46
Cylinders - Bore and stroke (in.) .... 4 @ 4 7/8 X 6 1/2
R.P.M. 850
Nebraska test number 206
Fuel tank capacity (gal.) 50
Final drive capacity (qt.) 10
Transmission capacity (qt.) 20
Crankcase capacity (qt.) 14
Cooling system capacity (gal.) 9 1/4
Grouser shoe height 2
Tracklink height 3 5/16
Roller outer flange O.D. 9 1/8
Roller inner flange O.D. 9 1/8
O.D. Rolling surface sprocket 8
Sprocket R.P.M. (2nd gear) 29.2
Valve clearance (hot) in .000" 15
Magneto points clearance in .000" .... 12 - 14
Options/Versions .... Wide, Orchard
Paint color .... Yellow

Model Forty

In 1934, the Model Forty replaced the Thirty Five in the product line. The Forty was produced until 1936 with a total number of 584 machines. Three versions of the Forty were available. These included the standard (or narrow-gauge) at 56 inches, wide-gauge at 74 inches and an orchard model. All variations of the Forty are rare and sought after by collectors. As with most of the early machines, no separate serial number was given to the special variations, making it difficult to tell how many of each were produced.

Model Forty

Serial Numbers .... 5G1 - 5G584
Manufacture Dates .... 12/5/34 - 8/10/36
Weight (lb.) 13310
Gauges .... 74 inch / 56 inch
Drawbar horsepower 44
Belt/PTO horsepower 52
Cylinders - Bore and stroke (in.) .... 4 @ 5 1/8 X 6 1/2
R.P.M. 850
Nebraska test number 244
Fuel tank capacity (gal.) 50
Final drive capacity (qt.) 10
Transmission capacity (qt.) 20
Crankcase capacity (qt.) 14
Cooling system capacity (gal.) 9 1/4
Grouser shoe height 2 1/8
Tracklink height 3 7/16
Roller outer flange O.D. 9 3/8
O.D. Rolling surface sprocket 8
Sprocket R.P.M. (2nd gear) 29.2
Valve clearance (hot) in .000" 12
Magneto points clearance in .000" 20
Options/Versions .... Wide, Orchard
Paint color .... Yellow

Model Fifty

The Model Fifty was introduced in 1931 to take its place in the product line as one of the company's larger tractors, weighing in at 18,080 pounds. When production ended in 1937, 1808 of the tractors had been produced; serial numbers ran from 5A1 to 5A1808.

The Model Fifty was available in standard (or narrow-gauge) at 60 inches as well as wide-gauge at 74 inches. It is unknown if any orchard models were produced. All variations of the Fifty are somewhat rare. The machines that are found missing parts or other components specific to this tractor are difficult to restore because this machine had many unique parts.

Some of the Model Fifty tractors had the Fifty designation located on the radiator side, while others had it located on the top. Early Model Fiftys, or machines made before 5A757, had the gas tank ahead of the operator. Machines made after that time had the fuel tank under the seat. The Model Fifty should be painted Highway Yellow with black decals and highlights.

The OHV engine produced 52 horsepower with a 5 1/2 x 6 1/2 inch bore and stroke. The cylinder heads of this tractor were individual and the intake and exhaust manifolds were located on opposite sides. This was a unique design at the time of this tractor's debut and makes the task of locating used parts difficult now.

Model Fifty

Serial Numbers .... 5A1 - 5A1808
Manufacture Dates .... 11/24/31 - 9/10/37
Weight (lb.) 18080
Gauges .... 74 inch / 60 inch
Drawbar horsepower 52
Belt/PTO horsepower 61
Cylinders - Bore and stroke (in.) .... 4 @ 5 1/2 X 6 1/2
R.P.M. 850
Nebraska test number 204
Fuel tank capacity (gal.) 60
Final drive capacity (qt.) 16
Transmission capacity (qt.) 32
Crankcase capacity (qt.) 14
Cooling system capacity (gal.) 11 1/2
Grouser shoe height 2 3/16
Tracklink height 4 3/8
Roller outer flange O.D. 10
Roller inner flange O.D. 10
O.D. Rolling surface sprocket 8 1/2
Sprocket R.P.M. (2nd gear) 25.4
Valve clearance (hot) in .000" 10
Magneto points clearance in .000" 20
Options/Versions .... Wide
Paint color .... Yellow

Model Sixty

The Caterpillar Sixty is one of the most widely known and recognized tractors of all time. Original production began in 1919 by the C. L. Best Company as a rival machine to the Holt 10-Ton. The Sixty quickly moved Best to the lead of the large crawler tractor market. In 1925, with the merger of these two companies, the Caterpillar Sixty remained the leader in large crawler tractor sales. When production ended in 1931, 13,516 tractors had been produced at the Peoria, Illinois, factory; 5,432 units were produced at the San Leandro, California, factory.

The Sixty was available in 72-inch standard-gauge and as a logging cruiser and snow-special model. Weighing in at 20,500 pounds, it was the largest tractor to be produced by the company at that time. The Sixty was powered by a 6 1/2 x 8 1/2 inch four-cylinder engine that produced 65 drawbar horsepower.

Model Sixty

Serial Numbers .... 101A - 5532A, PA1 - PA13516
Manufacture Dates .... 7/1/25 - 12/30/31
Weight (lb.) 20500
Gauges .... 72 inch
Drawbar horsepower 65
Belt/PTO horsepower 77
Cylinders - Bore and stroke (in.) .... 4 @ 6 1/2 X 8 1/2
R.P.M. 650
Nebraska test number 105
Fuel tank capacity (gal.) 70
Final drive capacity (qt.) 12
Transmission capacity (qt.) 32
Crankcase capacity (qt.) 20
Cooling system capacity (gal.) 38
Grouser shoe height 2 5/8
Sprocket R.P.M. (2nd gear) 25
Valve clearance (hot) in .000" 23
Magneto points clearance in .000" .... 12 - 14
Options/Versions .... Logging cruiser
Paint color .... Grey, Yellow after 12/7/31

Model Sixty Five

The Sixty Five tractor was introduced in 1932 as a modified version of the Model Sixty. The tractor was issued the serial number prefix 2D to 2D521. When production ceased in 1933, only 521 units had been produced.

The tractor weighed in at just 23,010 pounds with a 7 x 8 1/2 inch bore and stroke. The machine produced 73 drawbar horsepower and 84 belt horsepower. Standard track shoe width was 16 inches with other sizes available. The one gauge it was available in was 72 inches.

Model Sixty Five

Serial Numbers .... 2D1 - 2D521
Manufacture Dates .... 2/29/32 - 8/19/33
Weight (lb.) 23010
Gauges .... 72 inch
Drawbar horsepower 73
Belt/PTO horsepower 84
Cylinders - Bore and stroke (in.) .... 4 @ 7 X 8 1/2
R.P.M. 650
Nebraska test number 209
Fuel tank capacity (gal.) 90
Final drive capacity (qt.) 10
Transmission capacity (qt.) 32
Crankcase capacity (qt.) 26
Cooling system capacity (gal.) 40
Grouser shoe height 2 5/8
Sprocket R.P.M. (2nd gear) 25
Valve clearance (hot) in .000" 15
Magneto points clearance in .000" .... 12 - 14
Options/Versions .... Logging cruiser
Paint color .... Yellow

Model Seventy

In 1933, the year that the Model Sixty Five was discontinued, the Model Seventy was introduced. While the machine was produced for four years, only 266 units were produced. With this machine, the company resorted back to the old appearance of the machines and abandoned the new look that was given to the Sixty Five.

Like the Model Sixty Five, the Seventy is also a rare tractor. This machine was a victim of the new diesel engine that was slowly putting an end to the use of the spark-ignition engine in the large crawler tractors. The engine used was a 7 x 8 1/2 inch bore and stroke, four-cycle that still used the flywheel starting system.

The Model Seventy weighed in at approximately 31,000 pounds and produced 77 drawbar horsepower with test 213 at the Nebraska test site. Gauge to track center was 78 inches with a standard 20 inch track shoe, or grouser. It was also painted the now standard Highway Yellow and detailed in black. The Seventy was available in only 78 inch gauge.

Model Seventy

Serial Numbers .... 8D1 - 8D266
Manufacture Dates .... 2/6/33 - 2/18/37
Weight (lb.) 31070
Gauges .... 78 inch
Drawbar horsepower 77
Belt/PTO horsepower 89
Cylinders - Bore and stroke (in.) .... 4 @ 7 X 8 1/2
R.P.M. 700
Nebraska test number 213
Fuel tank capacity (gal.) 90
Final drive capacity (qt.) 26
Transmission capacity (qt.) 40
Crankcase capacity (qt.) 24
Cooling system capacity (gal.) 30
Grouser shoe height 2 5/8
Tracklink height 4 3/8
Roller outer flange O.D. .... 9 1/8 single flange
10 9/16 double flange
Roller inner flange O.D. 9 13/16
O.D. Rolling surface sprocket 8 13/16
Sprocket R.P.M. (2nd gear) 21.6
Valve clearance (hot) in .000" .... 17 - 23
Magneto points clearance in .000" 12
Paint color .... Yellow

R SERIES
GAS TRACTORS

Model R2 5E Series

In 1934, the three-speed Caterpillar R2 5E Series tractor was released. Similar to the wide-gauge Model Twenty Two tractor, the R2 sold in limited numbers. The tractor was only available in wide-gauge at 50 inches and probably was a government-designed machine.

Production of the R2 continued until 1937 with a total of 83 units being made. The R2 is listed as having 25 horsepower, which is about .8 horsepower less than the Twenty Two. While the engines of the two tractors are the same, the transmission gearing is vastly different. The gearing was changed through different sized gears. At least six gearing combinations were available.

Another unique feature of the R2 is the large cast-iron counterweights placed on each roller frame. Apparently this 350 pound casting was a government specification for either stability or traction. The castings are made in the shape of the dirt guards and have an indentation for the main spring to fit in. The military models were equipped with an odometer for either recording miles or speed. It was placed on a bracket near the clutch pedal with a hole drilled into the transmission bell housing. The forestry models have been found with a ring gear, starter and lighting generator. These options may have been specified by the agencies ordering the tractors.

Model R2 5E Series

Serial Numbers .... 5E3501 - 5E3583
Manufacture Dates .... 4/9/34 - 12/20/37
Weight (lb.) 6700
Gauges .... 50 inch
Drawbar horsepower 25
Belt/PTO horsepower 32
Cylinders - Bore and stroke (in.) .... 4 @ 4 X 5
R.P.M. 1250
Nebraska test number 220
Fuel tank capacity (gal.) 22
Final drive capacity (qt.) 4
Transmission capacity (qt.) 8
Crankcase capacity (qt.) 10
Cooling system capacity (gal.) 5
Grouser shoe height 1 7/8
Tracklink height 3
Roller outer flange O.D. 8
O.D. Rolling surface sprocket 7
Sprocket R.P.M. (2nd gear) 35
Valve clearance (hot) in .000" 12
Magneto points clearance in .000" 20
Options/Versions .... Wide
Paint color .... Yellow, Olive Drab

Model R2 J Series

The R2 5-speed (or J) Series, was introduced in July of 1938. Production of 1,150 wide-gauge (or 6J) and 1,185 narrow-gauge (or 4J) tractors ended in April 1942.

These tractors are nearly identical to the J model D2 tractors. The exception is that these R2 tractors were gas powered and had spark ignition.

The R2 J series is equipped with a four-cylinder, 3 3/4 x 5 engine producing 25 draw bar horsepower.

Sale of these machines was limited in the United States but the tractors seemed very popular in the United Kingdom. Many are in preservation there today.

Model R2 J Series

Serial Numbers .... 4J1 - 4J1185, 6J1 - 6J1150
Manufacture Dates .... 7/26/38 - 4/16/42
Weight (lb.) 6130
Gauges .... 4J = 40 inch / 6J = 50 inch
Drawbar horsepower 25
Belt/PTO horsepower 30
Cylinders - Bore and stroke (in.) .... 4 @ 3 3/4 X 5
R.P.M. 1525
Nebraska test number 320
Fuel tank capacity (gal.) 20
Final drive capacity (qt.) 4
Transmission capacity (qt.) 8
Crankcase capacity (qt.) 13
Cooling system capacity (gal.) 7
Grouser shoe height 1 7/8
Tracklink height 3
Roller outer flange O.D. 8
Roller inner flange O.D. 7 7/8
O.D. Rolling surface sprocket 7
Sprocket R.P.M. (2nd gear) 34
Valve clearance (hot) in .000" 15
Magneto points clearance in .000" 20
Options/Versions .... Wide, Orchard
Paint color .... Yellow

Model R3

In 1934, while the Model Twenty Eight tractor was being produced, a close companion to it, the Model R3, was introduced. The Model R3 was manufactured until 1935, with a total of 60 units produced. The serial numbers run from 5E2501 to 5E2560. By the small number produced, you can see this probably is the rarest of the small tractor line. It is unclear why so few of these tractors were produced, but it is probably due to the special government order. As with other unique models of limited production, such as the R2 5E Series, Diesel 70, D5 9M and R6, this may have been a government-originated design. The R3 was available only in the 55 inch wide-gauge, which was also the same width of the wide-gauge Twenty Eight.

The R3 was listed as producing 37 horsepower. This was six more horsepower than the Model Twenty Eight. The increase in horsepower was due to an increase in engine bore from 4 3/16 inches to 4 1/2 inches. The stroke of both tractors was 5 1/2 inches. The engine crankshaft is the same in both models, but the manifold, cylinders, block and head differ. The exhaust leaves the tractor at number one cylinder instead of the center of the manifold, as with the Model Twenty Eight.

Model R3

Serial Numbers .... 5E2501 - 5E2560
Manufacture Dates .... 4/1/34 - 11/30/35
Weight (lb.)... 9130
Gauges .... 55 inch
Drawbar horsepower 30
Belt/PTO horsepower 37
Cylinders - Bore and stroke (in.) .... 4 @ 4 1/2 X 5 1/2
R.P.M. 1100
Fuel tank capacity (gal.).. 25
Final drive capacity (qt.) 4
Transmission capacity (qt.) 8
Crankcase capacity (qt.)... 11
Cooling system capacity (gal.) 6
Grouser shoe height 1 7/8
Sprocket R.P.M. (2nd gear) 32
Valve clearance (hot) in .000" 15
Magneto points clearance in .000" 12
Options/Versions .... Wide
Paint color .... Yellow

Model R5

The Model R5 was introduced in 1934 during the end of the production run of the Thirty Five and at the beginning of the Forty's production. The R5 was made in three batches with a total production of 1,549 machines. The first series of the R5 was given the serial number prefix 5E, of which 500 units were produced. These first series machines had the most parts in common with the Thirty Five. The second series was the 4H Series, of which 1,000 units were produced. The tractors of this series likely have the most components in common with the Model Forty. The third series tractors were given the 3R serial number prefix, of which 49 units were produced. These machines, along with a portion of the 4H-designated machines, became the gasoline-fueled alternative to the RD6 tractor being produced during part of the same period. The R5 weighed 13,840 pounds.

Model R5

Serial Numbers 5E, 4H, 3R
Manufacture Dates .... 3/1/34 - 9/13/40
Weight (lb.) 13840
Gauges .... 74 inch / 56 inch
Drawbar horsepower 55
Belt/PTO horsepower 64
Cylinders - Bore and stroke (in.) .... 4 @ 5 1/2 X 6 1/2
R.P.M. 950
Nebraska test number 224
Fuel tank capacity (gal.) 50
Final drive capacity (qt.) 10
Transmission capacity (qt.) 20
Crankcase capacity (qt.) 14
Cooling system capacity (gal.) 9 1/4
Grouser shoe height 2 1/8
Tracklink height 3 7/16
Roller outer flange O.D. 9 1/8
Roller inner flange O.D. 9 1/8
O.D. Rolling surface sprocket 8
Sprocket R.P.M. (2nd gear) 29.2
Valve clearance (hot) in .000" 15
Magneto points clearance in .000" 20
Paint color .... Yellow

Model R6

The most mysterious tractor ever made may be the Model R6. Little is known about the machine except it was designed as the spark-ignition or gas-powered version of the Model RD6. Produced in 1941, it is not known if this tractor was issued a serial number. It is not known how many were produced or if they ever sold commercially. It is possible that the government is behind the origins of this machine.

It has been reported that some of these may have seen some service in the armed forces during World War II. In fact, two R6 tractors were possibly used in a logging operation on the West Coast some years back but were sold for scrap and apparently destroyed. It is not known if any survive at this time.

Weighing approximately 16,000 pounds, the R6 was available in 74 inch wide-gauge and 60 inch narrow-gauge. The tractor produced 55 drawbar horsepower and 65 belt horsepower.

There is no specifications sheet available for the Model R6.

NUMBERED SERIES DIESEL TRACTORS

Diesel Thirty Five

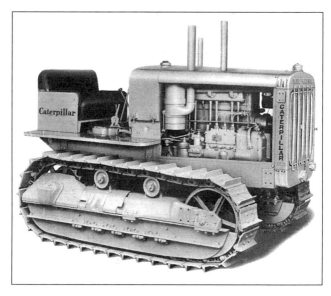

The Diesel Thirty Five was introduced in 1933, and was available in both 74 inch and 56 inch gauges. Production ended in 1934, with 1,999 machines sold. The Diesel Thirty Five was powered by a 5 1/4 x 8 inch diesel three-cylinder engine and produced 41 horsepower.

Diesel Thirty Five

Serial Numbers .... 6E1 - 6E1999
Manufacture Dates .... 7/19/33 - 10/23/34
Weight (lb.) 13900
Gauges .... 74 inch / 56 inch
Drawbar horsepower 41
Belt/PTO horsepower 46
Cylinders - Bore and stroke (in.) .... 3 @ 5 1/4 X 8
R.P.M. 850
Nebraska test number 217
Fuel tank capacity (gal.) 45
Final drive capacity (qt.) 10
Transmission capacity (qt.) 20
Crankcase capacity (qt.) 14
Cooling system capacity (gal.) 16
Grouser shoe height 2
Tracklink height 3 5/16
Roller outer flange O.D. 9 1/8
Roller inner flange O.D. 9 1/8
O.D. Rolling surface sprocket 8
Sprocket R.P.M. (2nd gear) 29.2
Valve clearance (hot) in .000" 12
Magneto points clearance in .000" .... 12 - 14
Options/Versions .... Wide, Orchard
Paint color .... Yellow

Diesel Forty

The Diesel Forty was introduced in 1934, and was available in both 74 inch and 56 inch gauges. Production ended in 1936, with 1,951 machines sold. The Diesel Forty was powered by a 5 1/4 x 8 inch diesel three-cylinder engine and produced 44 horsepower.

Diesel Forty

Serial Numbers .... 3G1 - 3G1951
Manufacture Dates .... 10/25/34 - 4/21/36
Weight (lb.) 14700
Gauges .... 74 inch / 56 inch
Drawbar horsepower 44
Belt/PTO horsepower 49
Cylinders - Bore and stroke (in.) .... 3 @ 5 1/4 X 8
R.P.M. 850
Nebraska test number 243
Fuel tank capacity (gal.) 45
Final drive capacity (qt.) 10
Transmission capacity (qt.) 20
Crankcase capacity (qt.) 14
Cooling system capacity (gal.) 16
Grouser shoe height 2 3/16
Tracklink height 3 7/16
Roller outer flange O.D. 9 3/8
Roller inner flange O.D. 9 1/8
O.D. Rolling surface sprocket 8
Sprocket R.P.M. (2nd gear) 29.2
Valve clearance (hot) in .000" 12
Magneto points clearance in .000" .... 12 - 14
Options/Versions .... Wide, Orchard
Paint color .... Yellow

Diesel Fifty

The Diesel Fifty was introduced in 1933, and was available in both 74 inch and 60 inch gauges. Production ended in 1936, with 2,062 machines sold. The Diesel Fifty was powered by a 5 1/4 x 8 inch four-cylinder diesel engine and produced 56 horsepower.

Diesel Fifty

Serial Numbers .... 1E1 - 1E2062
Manufacture Dates .... 3/4/33 - 2/27/36
Weight (lb.) 20250
Gauges .... 74 inch / 60 inch
Drawbar horsepower 56
Belt/PTO horsepower 66
Cylinders - Bore and stroke (in.) .... 4 @ 5 1/4 X 8
R.P.M. 850
Nebraska test number 214
Fuel tank capacity (gal.) 60
Final drive capacity (qt.) 16
Transmission capacity (qt.) 32
Crankcase capacity (qt.) 14
Cooling system capacity (gal.) 18 1/2
Grouser shoe height 2 3/16
Tracklink height 4 3/8
Roller outer flange O.D. 10
Roller inner flange O.D. 10
O.D. Rolling surface sprocket 8 1/2
Sprocket R.P.M. (2nd gear) 25.4
Valve clearance (hot) in .000" 12
Magneto points clearance in .000" 20
Options/Versions .... Wide
Paint color .... Yellow

Diesel Sixty/Sixty Five

The Diesel Sixty was introduced in 1931, and was available in a 72 inch gauge. Production ended in 1932, with 157 sold. The Diesel Sixty was powered by a 6 1/8 x 9 1/4 inch four-cylinder diesel engine that produced 70 horsepower.

Diesel Sixty/Sixty Five

Serial Numbers .... 1C1 - 1C157
Manufacture Dates .... 8/1/31 - 12/30/32
Weight (lb.) 24390
Gauges .... 72 inch
Drawbar horsepower 70
Belt/PTO horsepower 84
Cylinders - Bore and stroke (in.) .... 4 @ 6 1/8 X 9 1/4
R.P.M. 700
Nebraska test number 208
Fuel tank capacity (gal.) 75
Final drive capacity (qt.) 12
Transmission capacity (qt.) 32
Crankcase capacity (qt.) 24
Cooling system capacity (gal.) 38
Grouser shoe height 2 5/8
Sprocket R.P.M. (2nd gear) 25
Valve clearance (hot) in .000" 15
Magneto points clearance in .000" .... 12 - 14
Paint color .... Grey, Yellow after 12/7/31

Diesel Seventy

The Diesel Seventy was introduced in 1933, and was available in a 78 inch gauge. Production also ended in 1933, with 51 machines sold. The Diesel Seventy was powered by a 6 1/8 x 9 1/4 inch four-cylinder diesel engine which produced 76 horsepower.

It has also been found that possibly 26 of the 51 units produced were converted to Diesel Seventy Five tractors. The decision may have been made because the RPM of the Diesel Seventy was increased to 820 from 700 as it had been in the Diesel Sixty/Sixty Five. Perhaps the increase in RPM was too much for the D9900 to handle and the decision to convert the machines was made.

Diesel Seventy

Serial Numbers .... 3E1 - 3E51
Manufacture Dates .... 2/8/33 - 9/8/33
Weight (lb.) 30800
Gauges .... 78 inch
Drawbar horsepower 76
Belt/PTO horsepower 87
Cylinders - Bore and stroke (in.) .... 4 @ 6 1/8 X 9 1/4
R.P.M. 820
Final drive capacity (qt.) 26
Transmission capacity (qt.) 40
Crankcase capacity (qt.) 24
Cooling system capacity (gal.) 38
Grouser shoe height 2 5/8
Paint color .... Yellow

Diesel Seventy Five

The Diesel Seventy Five was introduced in 1933, and was available in a 78 inch gauge. Production ended in 1935, with 1,087 machines sold. The Diesel Seventy Five was powered by a 5 1/4 x 8 inch diesel six-cylinder engine and produced 83 horsepower.

Diesel Seventy Five

Serial Numbers .... 2E1 - 2E1087
Manufacture Dates .... 4/24/33 - 10/28/35
Weight (lb.) 32600
Gauges .... 78 inch
Drawbar horsepower 83
Belt/PTO horsepower 98
Cylinders - Bore and stroke (in.) .... 6 @ 5 1/4 X 8
R.P.M. 850
Nebraska test number 218
Fuel tank capacity (gal.) 69
Final drive capacity (qt.) 26
Transmission capacity (qt.) 40
Crankcase capacity (qt.) 28
Cooling system capacity (gal.) 28
Grouser shoe height 2 5/8
Tracklink height 4 3/4
Roller outer flange O.D. 9 1/8
O.D. Rolling surface sprocket 8 13/16
Sprocket R.P.M. (2nd gear) 21.6
Valve clearance (hot) in .000" 12
Magneto points clearance in .000" .... 12 - 14
Paint color .... Yellow

RD SERIES DIESEL TRACTORS

Model RD4

The model RD4 was introduced in 1936 and was the diesel powered version of the R4. It was available in 44 inch narrow and 60 inch wide-gauge. It was also available in an orchard model.

In 1939 the RD4 became the early model D4 at serial number 7J, the 2T and 5T followed suit in the same gauges. Other than the name the new machines were given, the overall machine stayed virtually the same. The D315 engine was not used in the D4 until the U series. The D4400 engine remained the Power unit for the RD4 and early D4.

Model RD4

Serial Numbers 4G, 7J, 2T, 5T
Manufacture Dates .... start 11/19/36
Weight (lb.) 10030
Gauges .... 60 inch / 44 inch
Drawbar horsepower 36
Belt/PTO horsepower 41
Cylinders - Bore and stroke (in.) .... 4 @ 4 1/4 X 5 1/2
R.P.M. 1400
Nebraska test number 273
Fuel tank capacity (gal.) 25
Final drive capacity (qt.) 7
Transmission capacity (qt.) 10
Crankcase capacity (qt.) 16
Cooling system capacity (gal.) 11
Grouser shoe height 2
Tracklink height 3 5/16
Roller outer flange O.D. 9 5/8
Roller inner flange O.D. 8 15/16
O.D. Rolling surface sprocket 8
Sprocket R.P.M. (2nd gear) 27
Valve clearance (hot) in .000" 10
Magneto points clearance in .000" 20
Options/Versions .... Wide, Orchard
Paint color .... Yellow

Model RD6

The RD6 tractor was introduced in 1935 in the 5E series. Only five tractors were produced with the 5E prefix. Production resumed the same year with the 2H series.

The tractor was re-designated the D6 around serial number 2H5100. These machines were known as the three-cylinder D6 tractors. When production ended in 1942, 8,966 RD6/D6 tractors were produced. It was available in 56 inch narrow-gauge and 74 inch wide-gauge. It replaced the Diesel Thirty Five and Forty tractors.

Model RD6

Serial Numbers 5E, 2H
Manufacture Dates .... 3/5/35 - 1/30/42
Weight (lb.) 15210
Gauges .... 74 inch / 56 inch
Drawbar horsepower 45
Belt/PTO horsepower 51
Cylinders - Bore and stroke (in.) .... 3 @ 5 3/4 X 8
R.P.M. 850
Nebraska test number 243
Fuel tank capacity (gal.) 45
Final drive capacity (qt.) 10
Transmission capacity (qt.) 20
Crankcase capacity (qt.) 14
Cooling system capacity (gal.) 16
Grouser shoe height 2 3/8
Tracklink height 3 7/16
Roller outer flange O.D. 9 3/8
Roller inner flange O.D. 8 13/16
O.D. Rolling surface sprocket 8
Sprocket R.P.M. (2nd gear) 29
Valve clearance (hot) in .000" 12
Magneto points clearance in .000" 20
Options/Versions .... Wide, Orchard
Paint color .... Yellow

Model RD7

The RD7 tractor was introduced in 1935 in the 5E series. Only 25 tractors were produced under the 5E prefix, until it was re-designated the same year as the 9G series.

Production of the RD7 continued until 1937 when the machine was re-named the D7 around serial number 9G2500.

Production ended in 1940 with 7,254 tractors made. It was available in 60 inch narrow and 74 inch wide-gauge. It replaced the Diesel Fifty.

Model RD7

Serial Numbers 9G
Manufacture Dates .... 1/30/35 - 1/25/40
Weight (lb.) 20490
Gauges .... 74 inch / 60 inch
Drawbar horsepower 69
Belt/PTO horsepower 82
Cylinders - Bore and stroke (in.) .... 4 @ 5 3/4 X 8
R.P.M. 850
Nebraska test number 254
Fuel tank capacity (gal.) 60
Final drive capacity (qt.) 16
Transmission capacity (qt.) 32
Crankcase capacity (qt.) 17
Cooling system capacity (gal.) 18 1/2
Grouser shoe height 2 3/16
Tracklink height 4 3/8
Roller outer flange O.D. 10
Roller inner flange O.D. 10
O.D. Rolling surface sprocket 8 1/2
Sprocket R.P.M. (2nd gear) 25
Valve clearance (hot) in .000" 12
Magneto points clearance in .000" 20
Options/Versions .... Wide
Paint color .... Yellow

Model RD8

The RD8 tractor was introduced in 1935 in the 5E series. Only 33 tractors were produced when it was issued the 1H prefix the same year.

In 1937 the RD8 was re-named the D8 around serial number 1H1500. Production ended in 1941 at serial number 1H9999. It was available in 78 inch gauge only. It replaced the Diesel Seventy Five tractor.

Model RD8

Serial Numbers 5E, 1H, 8R
Manufacture Dates .... 1/31/35 - 12/31/41
Weight (lb.) 33420
Gauges .... 78 inch
Drawbar horsepower .... 98 / 113
Belt/PTO horsepower .... 113 / 131
Cylinders - Bore and stroke (in.) .... 6 @ 5 3/4 X 8
R.P.M. 850
Nebraska test number 314
Fuel tank capacity (gal.) 69
Final drive capacity (qt.) 26
Transmission capacity (qt.) 40
Crankcase capacity (qt.) 27
Cooling system capacity (gal.) 28
Grouser shoe height 2 5/8
Tracklink height 4 3/8
Roller outer flange O.D. 10 9/16
Roller inner flange O.D. 9 13/16
O.D. Rolling surface sprocket 8 13/16
Sprocket R.P.M. (2nd gear) 22
Valve clearance (hot) in .000" 12
Magneto points clearance in .000" 20
Paint color .... Yellow

D Series Diesel Tractors

Model D2

The D2 was the smallest diesel tractor built by the company. It was first introduced in 1938 in the 3J series narrow-gauge (or 5J) series wide-gauge. Wide-gauge width was 50 inches and narrow-gauge was 40 inches.

When production of the J series machines ended in 1947, 8600 narrow (or 3J) machines were produced and 10,561 5J or wide-gauge. The "J" model D2 used the D3400 four-cylinder diesel engine.

In 1947 production of the U series D2 tractors began with the 4U narrow-gauge and 5U wide-gauge. The new machine was equipped with the D311 four-cylinder diesel engine. At serial numbers 4U6373 and 5U13237 many design changes occurred making the D2 a more user friendly and profitable tractor. Production ended in 1957 with 7560 4U units and 18,894 5U units.

The chart on the following page contains specifications for the 3J and 5J serial number ranges only.

Model D2

Serial Numbers 3J, 5J
Manufacture Dates .... 1938 - 1947
Weight (lb.) 6610
Gauges .... 5J = 50 inch / 3J = 40 inch
Drawbar horsepower 26
Belt/PTO horsepower 32
Cylinders - Bore and stroke (in.) .... 4 @ 3 3/4 X 5
R.P.M. 1525
Nebraska test number 322
Fuel tank capacity (gal.) 20
Final drive capacity (qt.) 4
Transmission capacity (qt.) 8
Crankcase capacity (qt.) 13
Cooling system capacity (gal.) 7 3/4
Grouser shoe height 1 7/8
Tracklink height 3
Roller outer flange O.D. 8
Roller inner flange O.D. 7 7/8
O.D. Rolling surface sprocket 7
Sprocket R.P.M. (2nd gear) 34
Valve clearance (hot) in .000" 10
Magneto points clearance in .000" 20
Options/Versions .... Wide, Orchard
Paint color .... Yellow

Model D4

The D4 tractor was transformed from the RD4 4G series in 1938. After production of the 7J, 2T, and 5T series tractors produced from 1939 to 1947, the new style D4 was introduced.

The U model D4 was available in the 6U series narrow-gauge, at 44 inches and 7U wide-gauge, at 60 inches.

The early RD4 was equipped with the D4400 four-cylinder engine as was the 7J, 2T, and 5T series. When the U model was introduced in 1947 it was equipped with the D315 engine. Production of both U model tractors ended in 1959 with 12,781 6U machines and 44,307 7U machines produced.

Model D4

Serial Numbers .... 6U1 - 6U12781, 7U1 - 7U44307
Manufacture Dates .... 1947 - 1959
Weight (lb.) 10500
Gauges .... 6U=44 inch / 7U=60 inch
Drawbar horsepower 43
Belt/PTO horsepower 48
Cylinders - Bore and stroke (in.) .... 4@ 4 1/2 X 5 1/2
R.P.M. 1400
Fuel tank capacity (gal.) 30
Final drive capacity (qt.) 7
Transmission capacity (qt.) 18
Crankcase capacity (qt.) 15
Cooling system capacity (gal.) 11
Grouser shoe height 1 7/8
Tracklink height 3 5/8
Sprocket R.P.M. (2nd gear) 27
Valve clearance (hot) in .000" 10
Magneto points clearance in .000" 20
Options/Versions .... Wide, Orchard
Paint color .... Yellow

See Model RD4 – page 67 – for specifications of early D4 tractors.

Model D5

The D5 9M series is a very mysterious tractor. It was most likely designed as a government order tractor in that only 46 were produced in 1939. It used a D4 chassis with a R series D6 engine. It was available only in 60 inch gauge.

Model D5

Serial Numbers 9M
Manufacture Dates .... 7/12/39 - 7/19/39
Weight (lb.) 11230
Gauges .... 60 inch
Drawbar horsepower 45
Belt/PTO horsepower 52
Cylinders - Bore and stroke (in.) .... 6 @ 4 1/4 X 5 1/2
R.P.M. 1400
Fuel tank capacity (gal.) 25
Final drive capacity (qt.) 7
Transmission capacity (qt.) 20
Crankcase capacity (qt.) 16
Cooling system capacity (gal.) 11
Grouser shoe height 2
Tracklink height 3 5/16
Roller outer flange O.D. 9 5/8
Roller inner flange O.D. 8 15/16
O.D. Rolling surface sprocket 8
Sprocket R.P.M. (2nd gear) 27
Valve clearance (hot) in .000" 12
Magneto points clearance in .000" 20
Options/Versions .... Wide
Paint color .... Yellow, (Unknown)

Model D6

The first six-cylinder D6 tractor was introduced in 1941 with the 4R and 5R series. This was the same engine used in the 9M D5 tractor. The 4R was wide-gauge at 74 inch and the 5R narrow-gauge at 60 inches. When production ended in 1947, 3,633 4R and 5,515 5R machines were produced.

Production of the D6 resumed in 1947 with the U series D6. The new D6 was installed with the four-cylinder D318 engine. The 8U series was narrow-gauge at 60 inches and 9U wide at 74 inches. Production continued until 1959 with 11,045 8U and 29,764 9U machines produced.

The chart on the following page contains specifications for the 4R and 5R serial number ranges only. Important differences for U series are outlined above.

Model D6

Serial Numbers 4R, 5R

Manufacture Dates ...... 3/17/41 - 12/31/43 - end of data

Weight (lb.) 16380

Gauges .... 4R = 74 inch / 5R = 60 inch

Drawbar horsepower 55

Belt/PTO horsepower 65

Cylinders - Bore and stroke (in.) .... 6 @ 4 1/4 X 5 1/2

R.P.M. 1400

Fuel tank capacity (gal.) 48

Final drive capacity (qt.) 12

Transmission capacity (qt.) 38

Crankcase capacity (qt.) 19

Cooling system capacity (gal.) 12 1/4

Grouser shoe height 2 1/8

Tracklink height 3 25/32

Roller outer flange O.D. 9 3/8

Roller inner flange O.D. 8 13/16

O.D. Rolling surface sprocket 8

Sprocket R.P.M. (2nd gear) 25

Valve clearance (hot) in .000" 10

Magneto points clearance in .000" 20

Options/Versions .... Wide

Paint color .... Yellow

See Model RD6 – page 69 – for specifications of early
D6 tractors.

Model D7

The new style D7 was introduced in 1940 in the 7M series. Production ended in 1944 with 9,999 7M D7 tractors produced.

Production continued the same year with the 3T serial number prefix. Production of the 3T ended in 1955 with 28,058 machines produced.

In 1944 and 1945, 9,999 4T series military D7 tractors were produced. All were available only in 74 inch gauge.

The chart on the following page contains specifications for the 7M serial number range only.

Model D7

Serial Numbers 7M
Manufacture Dates .... 1940 - 1944
Weight (lb.) 25925
Gauges .... 74 inch
Drawbar horsepower 81
Belt/PTO horsepower 93
Cylinders - Bore and stroke (in.) .... 4 @ 5 3/4 X 8
R.P.M. 1000
Fuel tank capacity (gal.) 65
Final drive capacity (qt.) 24
Transmission capacity (qt.) 40
Crankcase capacity (qt.) 22
Cooling system capacity (gal.) 18
Grouser shoe height 2 3/8
Tracklink height 4 1/2
Roller outer flange O.D. 10 1/4
Roller inner flange O.D. 9 5/8
O.D. Rolling surface sprocket 8 3/4
Sprocket R.P.M. (2nd gear) 22 1/2
Valve clearance (hot) in .000" 12
Magneto points clearance in .000" 20
Paint color .... Yellow

Model D8

The new style D8 production began in 1941 with the 8R series. Production of the 8R series continued until serial number 8R9999 in 1945 when production of the 2U began.

The 2U was produced until 1953 with 23,537 units produced. The D8 was available only in 78 inch gauge.

Model D8

Serial Numbers 2U
Weight (lb.) 36310
Gauges .... 78 inch
Drawbar horsepower 130
Belt/PTO horsepower 148
Cylinders - Bore and stroke (in.) .... 6 @ 5 3/4 X 8
R.P.M. 1000
Fuel tank capacity (gal.) 69
Final drive capacity (qt.) 26
Transmission capacity (qt.) 40
Crankcase capacity (qt.) 34
Cooling system capacity (gal.) 28
Grouser shoe height 2 5/8
Tracklink height 4 3/4
Roller outer flange O.D. 10 9/16
Roller inner flange O.D. 9 13/16
O.D. Rolling surface sprocket 8 13/16
Sprocket R.P.M. (2nd gear) 21
Valve clearance (hot) in .000" 12
Magneto points clearance in .000" 20
Paint color .... Yellow

See Model RD8 – page 73 – for specifications of 8R
series D8 tractors.

APPENDICES

DIESEL ENGINES

Diesel Engines

"CATERPILLAR"
D17000
ENGINE

8-CYLINDER DIESEL, V-TYPE

Brake horsepower, at 850 R.P.M.: Maximum, 160; for continuous sustained loads, 120. Bore and stroke, 5¾"x 8". R.P.M. (governed, at full load), 850. Starting method: Independent 2-cylinder, horizontal opposed, 4-stroke cycle gasoline engine. Fuel, Commercial Diesel Fuel.

"CATERPILLAR"
D13000
ENGINE

6-CYLINDER DIESEL

Brake horsepower, at 850 R.P.M.: Maximum, 125; for continuous sustained loads, 95. Bore and stroke, $5\frac{3}{4}''$ x 8''. R.P.M. (governed, at full load), 850. Starting method: Independent 2-cylinder, 4-stroke cycle gasoline engine. Fuel, Commercial Diesel Fuel.

"CATERPILLAR"
D11000
ENGINE

6-CYLINDER DIESEL

Brake horsepower, at 850 R.P.M.: Maximum, 100; for continuous sustained loads, 75. Bore and stroke, 5¼" x 8". R.P.M. (governed, at full load), 850. Starting method: Independent 2-cylinder, 4-stroke cycle gasoline engine. Fuel, Commercial Diesel Fuel.

"CATERPILLAR"
D8800
ENGINE

4-CYLINDER DIESEL

Brake horsepower, at 850 R.P.M.: Maximum, 80; for continuous sustained loads, 60. Bore and stroke, 5¾"x 8". R.P.M. (governed, at full load), 850. Starting method: Independent 2-cylinder, 4-stroke cycle gasoline engine. Fuel, Commercial Diesel Fuel.

"CATERPILLAR"
D7700
ENGINE

4-CYLINDER DIESEL

Brake horsepower, at 850 R.P.M.: Maximum, 66; for continuous sustained loads, 50. Bore and stroke, 5¼" x 8". R.P.M. (governed, at full load), 850. Starting method: Independent 2-cylinder, 4-stroke cycle gasoline engine. Fuel, Commercial Diesel Fuel.

"CATERPILLAR"
D6600
ENGINE

3-CYLINDER DIESEL

Brake horsepower, at 850 R.P.M.: Maximum, 60; for continuous sustained loads, 45. Bore and stroke, 5¾" x 8". R.P.M. (governed, at full load), 850. Starting method: Independent 2-cylinder, 4-stroke-cycle gasoline engine. Fuel, Commercial Diesel Fuel.

"CATERPILLAR" D4400 ENGINE

4-CYLINDER DIESEL

Brake horsepower, at 1400 R.P.M.: Maximum, 44; for continuous sustained loads, 33. Bore and stroke, 4¼" x 5½". R.P.M. (governed, at full load), 1,400. Starting method: Independent 2-cylinder, horizontal opposed, 4-stroke cycle gasoline engine. Fuel, Commercial Diesel Fuel.

High Clearance Tractors

Caterpillar High Clearance Tractors

In 1928 the first Model Ten tractors were produced. As production continued through the next two years, sales of the companies smallest tractor dropped.

In 1929 a prototype high clearance Model Ten was built at serial number PT2572. At the time this was done, apparently a decision was made to not go forward with the high clearance in production. It was not until the spring of 1931 that the high clearance Ten was introduced to salesmen in <u>The Dotted Line</u>. Approximately two months later it was introduced to customers in the Caterpillar Magazine.

For some time it was not known how many Model Ten tractors were high clearance. Early in the hobby it was speculated that 100 or less were produced. As the hobby grew, more and more high clearance Ten tractors surfaced to the point where some collectors even had more than one.

I had speculated in an earlier book that most likely 500 high Ten tractors were produced due to their excellent survival rate. I took into consideration that we knew for sure that only 95 1D series high Fifteen tractors were produced and only about six of them had surfaced.

High Clearance Ten

Recently, through extensive research by the Antique Caterpillar Machinery Owners Club directors, written documentation has been found that 397 high Ten tractors were produced in 1931. Most high

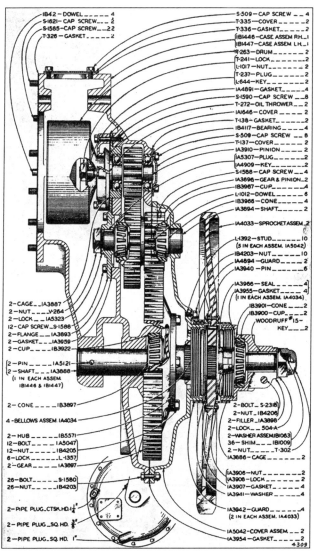

High Ten Final Drive

Ten tractors are in a group of tractors produced in 1930. It is thought the high Ten tractors were modified, in 1931, from 1930 production low Ten tractors that hadn't sold. It is also known the high Ten was made in a high wide version.

In 1932 the high Fifteen was introduced to replace the high Ten in the row crop market. The high Fifteen was issued serial number prefix 1D and 95 machines were produced. The high Fifteen was a 7C series or small Fifteen that was fitted with a clearance Ten undercarriage.

After introduction of the model Twenty Two it became the next tractor to be offered in the high clearance arrangement. According to Parts Catalog form #3525, the high clearance Twenty Two was only available in a high wide version. The parts book does not show a high narrow final as an option. The wide-gauge is created by use of a 2B7463 right hand spacer and a 2B7464 left hand spacer. It is feasible that the spacer acts more as an adapter than a spacer.

The high Twenty Two uses the same drive sprocket, rail, track roller frame and front idler as the high Ten. It is possible that the inside

1D Series High Clearance Fifteen

flange of the spacer is made to adapt to the Twenty Two final drive bolt pattern, while the outer flange bolts to the high Ten final drive bolt pattern. The final drive casting number for the high Ten and Twenty Two are however different.

Another interesting fact is that the Twenty Two high wide uses an "H" prefix in the serial number to identify it as a high clearance. Also, as part of the high clearance Twenty Two change-over group a different set of cylinder jugs were included. This group included the part number V-6 pistons. With this information I was able to determine that the cylinder bore on the high Twenty Two was decreased to 3 3/4 inches. This is 1/4 inch smaller than the 4 inch bore of the standard Twenty Two. The V-6 piston is the piston used in the PV Fifteen engine.

I believe the high clearance Twenty Two bore was decreased to 3 3/4 inches to lower the horsepower transmitted to the lighter duty high Ten drivetrain it used.

The Twenty Two does not appear to have been made in a group as the surviving high Twenty Two tractors are found throughout the product span bearing the letter "H" at the serial numbers end.

High Clearance Wide Twenty Two

High Wide Twenty Two (Both Photos)

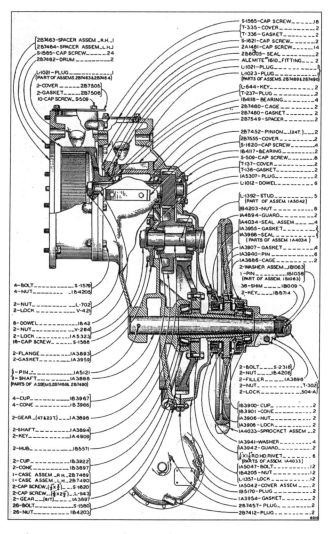

2B7463-SPACER ASSEM.-R.H._1
2B7464-SPACER ASSEM.-L.H._1
S-1585-CAP SCREW_____24
2B7462-DRUM _____2
L-1021-PLUG _
(PART OF ASSEMS.2B7463&2B7464)
2-COVER ____ 2B7505
2-GASKET____2B7506
10-CAP SCREW_S-509

S-1585-CAP SCREW_____18
T-335-COVER _____2
T-336-GASKET _____2
S-1621-CAP SCREW _____2
2A1481-CAP SCREW_____14
2B6005-SEAL _____2
ALEMITE "1610_FITTING__2
L-1021-PLUG _____
L-1023-PLUG _____
(PARTS OF ASSEMS.2B7489&2B7490)
L-644-KEY _____2
T-237-PLUG _____2
1B4118-BEARING _____4
2B7460-CAGE _____2
2B7480-GASKET _____2
2B7549-SPACER _____2

2B7452-PINION__(24T.)__2
2B7555-COVER _____2
S-1620-CAP SCREW_____4
1B4117-BEARING _____2
S-509-CAP SCREW_____8
T-137-COVER _____2
T-138-GASKET _____2
1A5307-PLUG _____2
L-1012-DOWEL _____6

L-1392-STUD _____5
(PART OF ASSEM.1A5042)
1B4203-NUT _____8
1A4894-GUARD _____2
1A4034-SEAL ASSEM.___4
1A3955-GASKET _____5
1A3966-SEAL _____
(PARTS OF ASSEM.1A4034)
1A3907-GASKET _____4
1A3940-PIN _____6
1A3886-CAGE _____2
2-WASHER ASSEM. 1B1063
1-PIN _____1B1058
(PART OF ASSEM.1B1063)
36-SHIM ___1B1009
2-KEY ___1B8714

4-BOLT _____S-1579
4-NUT _____1B4205

2-NUT _____L-702
2-LOCK _____V-421

8-DOWEL _____1B42
2-NUT _____V-264
2-LOCK _____1A5323
16-CAP SCREW ___S-1588

2-FLANGE _____1A3893
2-GASKET _____1A3959

1-PIN _____1A5121
1-SHAFT _____1A3888
(PARTS OF ASSEMS.2B7489& 2B7490)

4-CUP _____1B3967
4-CONE _____1B3966

2-GEAR _(47&23T.)__1A3896

2-SHAFT _____1A3894
2-KEY _____1A4909

2-HUB _____1B5571

2-CUP _____1B3922
2-CONE _____1B3897
1-CASE ASSEM._R.H._2B7489
1-CASE ASSEM._L.H._2B7490
2-CAP SCREW_(⅜x¾)__S-1620
2-CAP SCREW_(⅜x2½)__L-1143
2-GEAR _(61T)___1A3897
20-BOLT_____S-1580
26-NUT_____1B4203

2-BOLT___S-2318
2-NUT____1B4206
2-FILLER__1A3898
2-NUT____T-302
2-LOCK___504-A

1B3900-CUP _____2
1B3901-CONE _____2
1A3906-NUT _____2
1A3908-LOCK _____2
1A4033-SPROCKET ASSEM._2

1A3941-WASHER ____4
1A3942-GUARD ____2
¼x1¼RD.HD.RIVET__6
(PARTS OF ASSEM.1A4033)
1A5047-BOLT_____12
1B4205-NUT _____12
L-1357-LOCK _____12
1A5042-COVER ASSEM.__2
1B5170-PLUG _____2
1A3954-GASKET ____2
2B7457-PLUG _____2
2B7412-PLUG _____2

6016

High Twenty Two Final Drive Showing Spacers

105

VARIATIONS, OPTIONS, AND ACCESSORIES

Variations

8C Twenty Engine close-up

PV Fifteen with Cab as option

PV Fifteen Snow Special

Wide PV Fifteen with Swamp Pads as option

PV Fifteen Wide with Winch

PV Fifteen Canopy Top

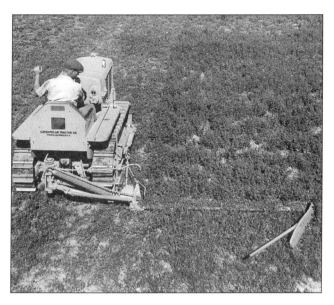

8C Twenty with cat Mower as option 4C series

PV Fifteen Orchard

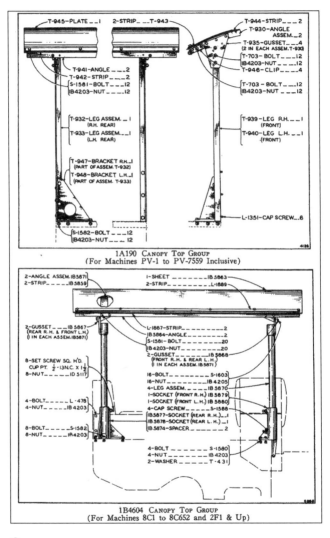

1A190 Canopy Top Group
(For Machines PV-1 to PV-7559 Inclusive)

1B4604 Canopy Top Group
(For Machines 8C1 to 8C652 and 2F1 & Up)

Canopy

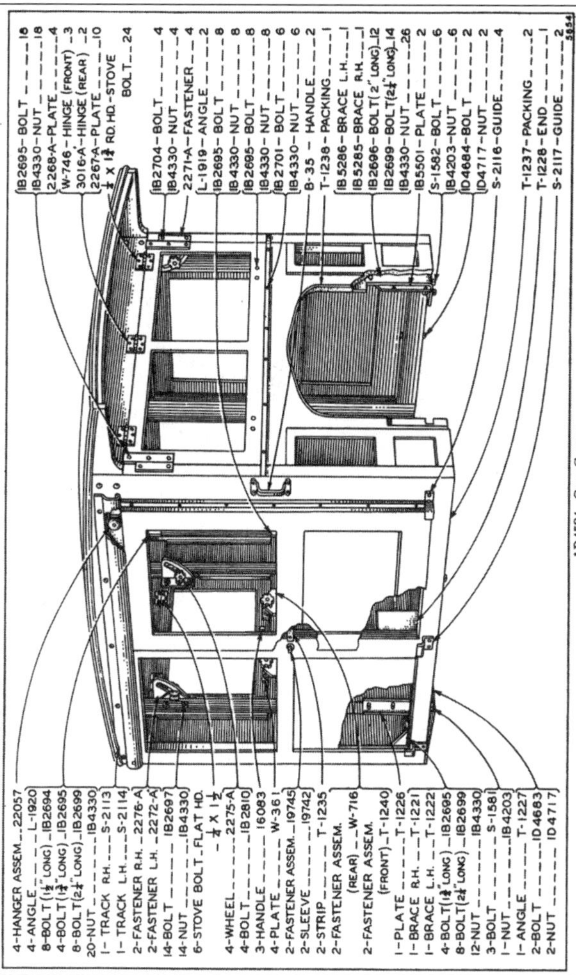
4-HANGER ASSEM.__22057
4-ANGLE ____ L-1920
8-BOLT (1½" LONG) _1B2694
4-BOLT (1¾" LONG) _1B2695
8-BOLT (2¼" LONG) _1B2699
20-NUT ______ 1B4330
1- TRACK R.H. ___S-2113
1- TRACK L.H. ___S-2114
2-FASTENER R.H. _2276-A
2-FASTENER L.H. _2272-A
14-BOLT ____ 1B2697
14-NUT _____ 1B4330
6-STOVE BOLT_FLAT HD. _¼ X 1½
4-WHEEL _____ 2275-A
4-BOLT _____ 1B2810
3-HANDLE ____ 16083
4-PLATE ____ W-361
2-FASTENER ASSEM._19745
2-SLEEVE _____ 19742
2-STRIP ____ T-1235
2-FASTENER ASSEM. (REAR) __W-716
2-FASTENER ASSEM. (FRONT)_T-1240
1-PLATE _____T-1226
1-BRACE R.H. __T-1221
1-BRACE L.H. __T-1222
4-BOLT (1¾" LONG) _1B2695
8-BOLT (2¼" LONG) _1B2699
12-NUT ______ 1B4330
3-BOLT _____ S-1581
1-NUT ______ 1B4203
1-ANGLE ____ T-1227
2-BOLT _____ 1D4683
2-NUT _____ 1D4717
1B2695- BOLT ____ 18
1B4330-NUT _____ 18
2268-A-PLATE _____ 4
W-746 - HINGE (FRONT) _3
3016-A - HINGE (REAR) _2
2267-A-PLATE ____ 10
¼ X 1¾ RD. HD.-STOVE BOLT__24
1B2704-BOLT ____ 4
1B4330-NUT _____ 4
2271-A-FASTENER __ 4
L-1919-ANGLE ____ 2
1B2695- BOLT _____ 8
1B4330-NUT _____ 8
1B2695- BOLT _____ 8
1B4330- NUT _____ 8
1B2701- BOLT _____ 6
1B4330-NUT _____ 6
B-35 - HANDLE ___ 2
T-1238-PACKING ____ 1
1B5286-BRACE L.H.___ 1
1B5285-BRACE R.H.___ 1
1B2696-BOLT (2" LONG)_12
1B2699-BOLT (2¼" LONG)_14
1B4330-NUT _____ 26
1B5501-PLATE ____ 2
S-1582-BOLT _____ 6
1B4203-NUT _____ 6
1D4684-BOLT ____ 2
1D4717-NUT _____ 2
S-2116-GUIDE _____ 4
T-1237-PACKING ____ 2
T-1228-END _____ 1
S-2117-GUIDE ____ 2
5854

1B4594 Cab Group
(For Machines 8C1 to 8C652 Inclusive)

Cab Group

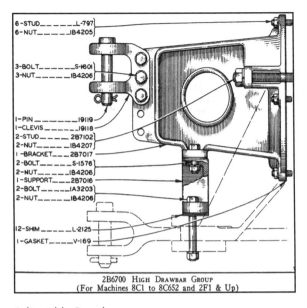

6-STUD_____L-797
6-NUT_____IB4205

3-BOLT_____S-1601
3-NUT_____IB4206

1-PIN_____19119
1-CLEVIS_____19118
2-STUD_____2B7102
2-NUT_____IB4207
1-BRACKET_____2B7017
2-BOLT_____S-1576
2-NUT_____IB4206
1-SUPPORT_____2B7016
2-BOLT_____IA3203
2-NUT_____IB4206

12-SHIM_____L-2125
1-GASKET_____V-169

2B6700 High Drawbar Group
(For Machines 8C1 to 8C652 and 2F1 & Up)

Adjustable Drawbar

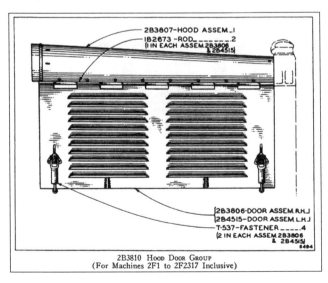

2B3807-HOOD ASSEM.1
IB2673-ROD_____2
(1 IN EACH ASSEM.2B3806
& 2B4515)

2B3806-DOOR ASSEM.R.H.1
2B4515-DOOR ASSEM.L.H.1
T-537-FASTENER_____4
(2 IN EACH ASSEM.2B3806
& 2B4515)

2B3810 Hood Door Group
(For Machines 2F1 to 2F2317 Inclusive)

Hood and Side Curtains

114

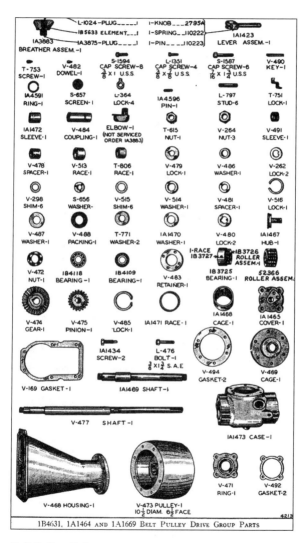

L-1024 – PLUG_____1
IB 5633 ELEMENT____1
1A3883   1A3875 – PLUG____1
BREATHER ASSEM.-1

I-KNOB____2795A
I-SPRING___110222
I-PIN____110223
1A1423
LEVER ASSEM.-1

T-753
SCREW-1

V-482
DOWEL-I

S-1594
CAP SCREW-8
$\frac{3}{8}$ X 1 U.S.S.

L-1351
CAP SCREW-4
$\frac{3}{8}$ X $\frac{7}{8}$ U.S.S.

S-1587
CAP SCREW-6
$\frac{7}{16}$ X 1$\frac{3}{4}$ U.S.S.

V-490
KEY-I

1A4591
RING-I

S-657
SCREEN-1

L-364
LOCK-4

1A4596
PIN-I

L-797
STUD-6

T-751
LOCK-I

1A1472
SLEEVE-I

V-484
COUPLING-I

ELBOW-1
(NOT SERVICED
ORDER 1A3883)

T-615
NUT-I

V-264
NUT-3

V-491
SLEEVE-I

V-478
SPACER-I

V-513
RACE-I

T-806
RACE-I

V-479
LOCK-I

V-486
WASHER-I

V-262
LOCK-2

V-298
SHIM-6

S-656
WASHER-

V-515
SHIM-6

V-514
WASHER-I

V-481
SPACER-I

V-516
LOCK-I

V-487
WASHER-I

V-488
PACKING-I

T-771
WASHER-2

1A1470
WASHER-I

V-480
LOCK-2

1A1467
HUB-I

V-472
NUT-I

1B4118
BEARING-I

1B4109
BEARING-I

V-483
RETAINER-I

I-RACE
1B3727—IB3726
ROLLER
ASSEM.-I
1B3725
BEARING-I

52366
ROLLER ASSEM.

V-474
GEAR-I

V-475
PINION-I

V-485
LOCK-I

1A1471 RACE-I

1A1468
CAGE-I

1A1465
COVER-I

1A1434
SCREW-2

L-476
BOLT-I
$\frac{9}{16}$ X 1$\frac{3}{4}$ S.A.E.

V-494
GASKET-2

V-469
CAGE-I

V-169 GASKET-I

1A1469 SHAFT-I

V-477   SHAFT-I

1A1473 CASE-I

V-468 HOUSING-I

V-473 PULLEY-I
10$\frac{1}{2}$ DIAM. 6$\frac{1}{2}$ FACE

V-471
RING-I

V-492
GASKET-2

4213

1B4631, 1A1464 AND 1A1669 BELT PULLEY DRIVE GROUP PARTS

Belt Pulley Drive

ADDITIONAL CHARTS

Caterpillar Carburetor Applications

Years		Engine	Tractor Model	Carburetor	Type
			Starting engines	Ensign	BeVd
			R3	Ensign	Ke 1.25
			R5	Ensign	Ked 1.5
			40	Ensign	K3
				Zenith	
				Zenith	
				Zenith	261-8
			UV-461, UV-549	Zenith	261-8
			Starting engines	Ensign	BeVc
1922				Kingston	L2V
1922				Kingston	L3
1923				Kingston	L3
1924		4	30	Stromberg	MP-3
1924		4	60	Stromberg	M-4
1925	1931	4	60	Ensign	AeLC 1.25
1925	1927	4	30	Ensign	Ae 1.5
1925	1931	4	30	Ensign	AeS 1.25
1925	1931	4	60	Ensign	AAe 1.75
1925	1931	4	60	Ensign	Ae 1.75
1927				Kingston	L3
1928	1932	4	20	Ensign	BeVb (R)
1928	1932	4	20	Ensign	AeL 1.25
1928	1932	4	20	Ensign	AeLC 1.25
1928	1932	4	20	Ensign	BeV
1929	1931	4	10	Ensign	BeT 1
1929	1931	4	10	Ensign	BeTb (R)
1929	1932	4	15	Ensign	BeV
1929	1932	4	15	Ensign	BeVb (R)
1929	1931	4	15, 15HC	Ensign	BeT 1
1929	1932	4	15	Ensign	BeTb (R)
1932	1934		35	Ensign	AeSd 1.25
1932	1934		35	Ensign	Kec 1.25
1932	1937		50	Ensign	Ke 1.5
1932	1934		35	Ensign	AeSc 1.25
1932			65	Ensign	Ke 1.75
1932		4	25	Ensign	AeLC 1.25
1934			22	Ensign	Ked 1.25
1934			22 Alcohol	Zenith	K5A
1934	1937		50 Alcohol	Zenith	K6A

Years		Engine	Tractor Model	Carburetor	Type
1934			RD7, 75	Zenith	IN194.5 X
1934	1936	4	70	Ensign	Keb 1.75
1935	1936		22 (Fuel oil)	Zenith	K5A
1936	1943		22	Zenith	K5A
1936	1943		R5	Zenith	K6A
1936	1943		R4	Zenith	K5A
1936	1943		50	Zenith	K5A
1936			D2, D4 (Starting)	Zenith	TU4C
1937	1939		D6, D8, RD7, D11000	Zenith	22AX8
1938			R2	Ensign	Ked 1.25
1938	1943		R2, 8 (Grader)	Zenith	K5A
1939			D7 (Starting)	Zenith	22AX8
1940	1946		D7 (Starting)	Zenith	22AX8
1940	1946		D4 (Starting)	Zenith	TU4C
1940	1944		D6, D8, RD7 (Starting)	Zenith	22AX8
1940			D2, D4 (Starting)	Zenith	TU4C
1941	1946		D2, D4 (Starting)	Zenith	TU4C
1941	1946		R6	Zenith	K5A
1941	1944		B	Zenith	IN93.5H
1941			R2, T72 Fuel Oil	Zenith	K5A
1941			R4, #10, #112 Fuel Oil	Zenith	K5A
1942	1944		Army Tractor (Starting)	Zenith	22AX8
1946	1950		D2, D4	Zenith	TU4C
1946	1948		D2	Zenith	TU4C
1946	1948		D2	Zenith	TU4C
1946	1959		D2	Zenith	TU4C
1946	1961		D4600 Starting Engine	Zenith	TU4C
1946	1952		D7	Zenith	22AX8
1946	1950		D4	Zenith	TU4C
1946	1952		D6, D8, RD7	Zenith	22AX8
1950			RM62, RM82	Zenith	261-8
1951			DW20, DW21	Zenith	261-8
1952			DW21	Zenith	261-8
1954	1958		D6, D7, D8	Zenith	261-8
1957	1961		D2, 212, D311, 922	Zenith	TU3.5XIC
1957				Zenith	261-8
1958	1961			Zenith	261-8
1958	1959		D9	Zenith	261-8
1958	1959		D2, 212, D311, 922	Zenith	TU3.5XIC
1959	1961			Zenith	TU3.5XIC
1959	1961		D4, 944, 955, 966	Zenith	TU4C
1959	1960			Zenith	261-8
1960	1961		D7, D8, 572, 583	Zenith	261-8
1960	1961			Zenith	TU4C
1960	1961		977	Zenith	TU4C

Chart of Specifications

SIZE	SERIAL NUMBER IDENTIFICA- TION (a)	MAXIMUM DRAWBAR HORSE POWER (a)	MAXIMUM BELT HORSE POWER (a)	SHIPPING WEIGHT (Pounds) (d)
Diesel Seventy-Five	2E1	83.23	98.01	32600
Diesel Seventy	3E3	76.00	87.00	30800
Seventy	8D1	77.07	89.43	31070
Diesel Sixty-Five	1C1	70.25	83.86	24390
Sixty-Five	2D1	73.33	83.66	23010
D7 (RD7)	5E7501, 9G1	69.41	82.04	20490
Sixty	101A, PA1	65.60	77.10	20500
R6 (RD6)	5E8501, 2H1	44.75	51.86	15210
D6	4R1, 5R1	55.00	65.00	16695
Diesel Fifty	1E1	56.03	65.60	20250
Fifty	5A1	51.96	60.75	18080
R5	5E3001 4H501, 3R1	54.99	64.28	13840
Diesel Forty	3G1	44.00	49.00	14700
Forty	5G1	44.19	51.53	13310
Diesel Thirty-Five	6E1	40.95	46.15	13900
Thirty-Five	5C1	38.6	46.08	12480
Thirty	S5001, PS1	35.6	40.2	9910
D4 (RD4)	4G1-2T1 7J1-5T1	35.68	41.17	10195
R4	6G1	35.33–32.39(a)	40.83–37.97 (a)	9390
Twenty-Eight	4F1	30.49–25.00 (a)	37.47–31.00 (a)	7830
Twenty-Five	3C1	28.63	35.18	7707
Twenty-Two	2F1, 1J1	25.79–25.15 (a)	31.96–31.47 (a)	6210
R3	5E2501	36.61	43.88	9130
R2	5E3501 6J1, 4J1	25.06–24.66(a)	31.07–30.82(a)	6130
D2	3J1, 5J1	25.86	31.99	6710
Twenty	L1, PL1	28.03	31.16	7740
Twenty (Repl. Fifteen)	8C1	23.69	28.39	5933
Fifteen	PV1	22.77	25.94	5790
Fifteen (Replaced Ten)	7C1	18.03	21.63	4480
High-Clearance Fifteen	1D1	18.03	21.63	5050
Ten	PT1	15.15	18.72	4420
High-Clearance Ten	PT1	15.15	18.72	5020

(a) These values are maximum load test data corrected to sea level barometric pres-
sure (29.92° Hg.) and standard temperature of 60° F. as outlined in the A.S.A.E.
and S.A.E. test codes. University of Nebraska official tractor test report data
have been used where available. Where two figures are given the first one refers
to operation on gasoline and the second to operation on tractor fuels.

Chart of Specifications

SIZE	SPEED IN M.P.H. AT FULL LOAD GOVERNED ENGINE R.P.M.							
	First	Second	Third	Fourth	Fifth	Sixth	Reverse Low	Reverse High
Diesel Seventy-Five	1.7	2.4	2.8	3.2	3.9	5.3	1.7	2.8
Diesel Seventy	1.7	2.3	2.7	3.1	3.7	5.0	1.7	2.7
Seventy	1.7	2.3	2.7	3.1	3.7	5.0	1.7	2.7
Diesel Sixty-Five	2.1	2.8	4.7	X	X	X	2.3	X
Sixty-Five	1.9	2.6	4.4	X	X	X	2.1	X
D7 (RD7)	1.6	2.4	3.4	4.7	X	X	1.9	X
Sixty	1.9	2.6	3.7	X	X	X	1.4	X
R6 (RD6)	1.7	2.5	3.2	4.6	X	X	1.9	X
D6	1.4	2.3	3.2	4.4	5.8	X	1.8	5.4
Diesel Fifty	1.6	2.4	3.4	4.7	X	X	1.9	X
Fifty	1.6	2.4	3.4	4.7	X	X	1.9	X
R5	1.9	2.8	3.6	5.1	X	X	2.1	X
Diesel Forty	1.7	2.5	3.2	4.6	X	X	1.9	X
Forty	1.7	2.5	3.2	4.6	X	X	1.9	X
Diesel Thirty-Five	1.7	2.5	3.2	4.6	X	X	1.9	X
Thirty-Five	1.7	2.5	3.2	4.6	X	X	1.9	X
Thirty	1.7	2.6	3.6	X	X	X	2.0	X
D4 (RD4)	1.7	2.4	3.0	3.7	5.4	X	1.9	X
R4	1.7	2.4	3.0	3.7	5.4	X	1.9	X
Twenty-Eight	1.8	2.6	3.6	X	X	X	2.0	X
Twenty-Five	1.8	2.6	3.6	X	X	X	2.0	X
Twenty-Two	2.0	2.6	3.6	X	X	X	2.1	X
R3	1.8	2.6	3.6	X	X	X	2.0	X
R2	1.7	2.5	3.0	3.6	5.1	X	2.1	X
D2	1.7	2.5	3.0	3.6	5.1	X	2.1	X
Twenty	1.8 (c)	2.6	3.6	X	X	X	2.0	X
Twenty (Repl. Fifteen)	2.0	2.6	3.6	X	X	X	2.1	X
Fifteen	2.0	2.6	3.6	X	X	X	2.1	X
Fifteen (Replaced Ten)	2.0	2.6	3.5	X	X	X	2.1	X
High-Clearance Fifteen	2.0	2.6	3.5	X	X	X	2.1	X
Ten	2.0	2.6	3.5	X	X	X	2.1	X
High-Clearance Ten	2.0	2.6	3.5	X	X	X	2.1	X

(b) Not tested at University of Nebraska.
(c) Speeds different than when machine was tested.
(d) Standard or narrow gauge.

NOTE: (____X____ signifies information not available because of machine design.

Chart of Specifications

SIZE	MAXIMUM DRAWBAR PULL POUNDS AT RATED ENGINE SPEED (e)					
	First	Second	Third	Fourth	Fifth	Sixth
Diesel Seventy-Five	18697	13334	10985	9311	7346	5196
Diesel Seventy	17200	12400	10410	8690	6975	4630
Seventy	16796	11790	9528	8228	6453	4403
Diesel Sixty-Five	11991	8817	4449	X	X	X
Sixty-Five	13597	9906	4950	X	X	X
D7 (RD7)	16098	10236	6792	4564	X	X
Sixty	12360	9155	6240	X	X	X
R6 (RD6)	10753	7238	5230	3261	X	X
D6	15850	10100	6880	4440	2950	X
Diesel Fifty	12765	7751	5145	3305	X	X
Fifty	12061	7457	4996	3337	X	X
R5	10384	6778	5049	3288	X	X
Diesel Forty	9692	6524	4714	2939	X	X
Forty	9496	6321	4613	3086	X	X
Diesel Thirty-Five	9135	5966	4303	2716	X	X
Thirty-Five	8169	5542	4005	2574	X	X
Thirty	7563	4823	3343	X	X	X
D4 (RD4)	8637	6392	4955	3818	2453	X
R4	7211–6120(a)	5186–4264(a)	4105–3642(a)	3147–2536(a)	2045–1680(a)	X
Twenty-Eight	6810–5880(a)	4578–3750(a)	3100–2550(a)	X	X	X
Twenty-Five	6011	4068	2746	X	X	X
Twenty-Two	4900–4534(a)	3705–3294(a)	2448–2214(a)	X	X	X
R3	7927	5459	3712	X	X	X
R2	6150–5150(a)	4380–4270(a)	3570–3330(a)	2970–2760(a)	1860–1740(a)	X
D2	6680	4420	3570	2890	1840	X
Twenty	6259	4208	2851	X	X	X
Twenty (Repl. Fifteen)	4572	3486	2375	X	X	X
Fifteen	4166	3175	2039	X	X	X
Fifteen (Replaced Ten)	3315	2657	1818	X	X	X
High-Clearance Fifteen	3315	2657	1818	X	X	X
Ten	2816	2087	1455	X	X	X
High-Clearance Ten	2947	2197	1521	X	X	X

(e) Observed drawbar pull as reported in Nebraska Tractor Tests except where later tractors had different gear ratios with same engine as the machine tested, or where tractors were not tested. In these cases the maximum drawbar pounds pull is based on maximum drawbar horsepower.

Chart of Specifications

SIZE	NEBRASKA TEST NO.	GAUGES (f)	ENGINE		
			Type	No. Cylinders @ Bore x Stroke	R. P. M. Governed at Full Load
Diesel Seventy-Five	218	78"	V. I. H.	6@5¼"x8"	850 (g)
Diesel Seventy	(b)	78"	V. I. H.	4@6⅛"x9¼"	820
Seventy	213	78"	V. I. H.	4@7 "x8½"	700
Diesel Sixty-Five	208	72"	V. I. H.	4@6⅛"x9¼"	700
Sixty-Five	209	72"	V. I. H.	4@7 "x8½"	650
D7 (RD7)	254 (h)	74"–60"	V. I. H.	4@5¾"x8"	850
Sixty	105	72"	V. I. H.	4@6½"x8½"	650
R6 (RD6)	243	74"–56"	V. I. H.	3@5¾"x8"	850
D6	(b)	74"–60"	V. I. H.	6@4¼"x5½"	1400
Diesel Fifty	214	74"–60"	V. I. H.	4@5¼"x8"	850
Fifty	204	74"–60"	V. I. H.	4@5½"x6½"	850
R5	224	74"–56"	V. I. H.	4@5½"x6½"	950
Diesel Forty	243	74"–56"	V. I. H.	3@5¼"x8"	850
Forty	244	74"–56"	V. I. H.	4@5⅛"x6½"	850
Diesel Thirty-Five	217	74"–56"	V. I. H.	3@5¼"x8"	850
Thirty-Five	206	74"–56"	V. I. H.	4@4⅞"x6½"	850
Thirty	104	60¾"–43¾"	V. I. H.	4@4¾"x6½"	850
D4 (RD4)	273	60"–44"	V. I. H.	4@4¼"x5½"	1400
R4	272–271	60"–44"	V. I. H.	4@4¼"x5½"	1400
Twenty-Eight	(b)	55"–42"	V. I. H.	4@4 3/16"x5½"	1100
Twenty-Five	203	55"–42"	V. I. H.	4@4 "x5½"	1100
Twenty-Two	228–226 (a)	50"–40"	V. I. H.	4@4 "x5"	1250
R3	227	55"	V. I. H.	4@4½x5½"	1100
R2	320–321	50"–40"	V. I. H.	4@3¾"x5"	1525
D2	322	50"–40"	V. I. H.	4@3¾"x5"	1525
Twenty	150	55"–42"	V. I. H.	4@4 "x5½"	1100
Twenty (Repl. Fifteen)	205	50"–40"	L-Head	4@3¾"x5"	1250
Fifteen	159	50"–40"	L-Head	4@3¾"x5"	1250
Fifteen (Replaced Ten)	207	44"–37"	L-Head	4@3⅜"x4"	1500
High-Clearance Fifteen	(b)	44"	L-Head	4@3⅜"x4"	1500
Ten	160	44"–37"	L-Head	4@3⅜"x4"	1500
High-Clearance Ten	(b)	44"	L-Head	4@3⅜"x4"	1500

(f) Center to center of tracks—the figure or figures are the gauge or gauges in which the tractor was available.
(g) Speed changed since tested at Nebraska.
(h) See also Tests Nos. 253 and 255.

Serial Number chart

From	To	Model Name
1C1	1C157	Diesel Sixty/Sixty Five
1D1	1D95	Fifteen Tractor Hi-Clearance
1E1	1E2062	Diesel Fifty Tractor
1H1	1H9999	D8 Tractor
1J1	1J5155	Twenty Two Tractor
2D1	2D521	Sixty Five Tractor (Gasoline)
2E1	2E1087	Diesel Seventy Five Tractor
2F1	2F9999	Twenty Two Tractor
2H1	2H8966	D6 Tractor
2T1	2T9999	D4 Tractor
2U1	Up	D8 Tractor
3C1	3C638	Twenty Five Tractor
3E1	3E51	Diesel Seventy Tractor
3G1	3G1951	Diesel Forty Tractor
3J1	3J8600	D2 Tractor
3R1	3R49	R5 Tractor
3T1	Up	D7 Tractor
4F1	4F1171	Twenty Eight Tractor
4G1	4G9999	D4 Tractor
4H501	4H1500	R5 Tractor
4J1	4J1185	R2 Tractor
4R1	4R3633	D6 Tractor (74" Gauge)
4T1	4T9999	D7 Tractor
4U1	Up	D2 Tractor (40" Gauge)
5C1	5C1728	Thirty Five Tractor
5E2501	5E2560	R3 Tractor
5E3001	5E3500	R5 Tractor
5E3501	5E3583	R2 Tractor
5E7501	5E7525	D7 Tractor
5E8001	5E8035	D8 Tractor
5E8501	5E8505	D6 Tractor
5G1	5G584	Forty Tractor
5J1	5J10561	D2 Tractor Wide Gauge
5R1	5R5515	D6 Tractor (60" Gauge)
5T1	5T7411	D4 Tractor
5U1	Up	D2 Tractor (50" Gauge)
6E1	6E1999	Diesel Thirty Five Tractor
6G1	6G5383	Thirty Tractor
6J1	6J1150	R2 Tractor Wide Gauge
6T1	6T1054	D7 Tractor
6U1	Up	D4 Tractor (44" Gauge)
7C1	7C307	Fifteen Tractor
7J1	7J9999	D4 Tractor
7M1	7M9999	D7 Tractor
7U1	Up	D4 Tractor (60" Gauge)
8C1	8C652	Twenty Tractor
8D1	8D266	Seventy Tractor (Gasoline)
8R1	8R9999	D8 Tractor
8U1	Up	D6 Tractor (60" Gauge)
9G1	9G7254	D7 Tractor
9M1	9M46	D5 Tractor
9U1	Up	D6 Tractor (74" Gauge)
L-1	L-1970	Twenty Tractor
PA-1	PA-13516	Sixty Tractor
PL-1	PL-6319	Twenty Tractor
PL-6587	PL-6598	Twenty Tractor
PS-1	PS-14294	Thirty Tractor
PT-1	PT-4929	Ten Tractor
PV-1	PV-7559	Fifteen Tractor
S-1001	S-10536	Thirty Tractor

Clubs

Antique Caterpillar Machinery Owners Club
PO Box 2220
East Peoria, IL 61611
(309) 694-0664
www.acmoc.org
email: cat@acmoc.org
Available from the club is the reference book:
Track-Type Machines 1925-1960 Serial Number Manual
A year by year guide to Caterpillar tracked machinery serial numbers.

Historic Construction Equipment Association
16623 Liberty Hi Road
Bowling Green, OH 43402
www.bigtoy.com

About the Author

Experienced author and renowned Caterpillar historian, Bob LaVoie, has been a Caterpillar enthusiast since the age of 15 when he bought his first Caterpillar road grader.

Bob worked first as a paramedic and then in road construction as a heavy equipment operator. Today, Bob resides in Park Falls, Wisconsin and spends his time collecting and restoring Caterpillar tractors.

Bob has previously authored five books including:

Caterpillar Gas Tractor Restoration and Interchange Manual: Model 10 to 70

Caterpillar Thirty Photo Archive, 2nd Edition including Best Thirty, 6G Thirty & R4

Caterpillar D-2 & R-2 Photo Archive

Caterpillar D-8 1933-1974 Photo Archive including Diesel Seventy-Five & RD-8

Caterpillar Ten Photo Archive including 7C Fifteen and High Fifteen.

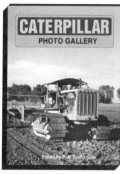

More Great Books
from **Iconografix!**

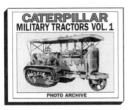

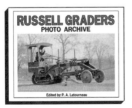